Mama's Legacy Series
Volume VII – 4th Edition

Sauce Recipes
50 Tasty Choices

Nancy N. Wilson

Sauce Recipes
50 Tasty Choices

Mama's Legacy Series
Volume VII – 4th Edition – October 2013
© Blurtigo Holdings, LLC

First Published 2012 in United States of America
ISBN-13: 978-1482530735

Disclaimer and Terms of Use: The Author and Publisher have strived to be as accurate and complete as possible in the creation of this book. While all attempts have been made to verify information provided in this publication, the Author and Publisher assume no responsibility for errors, omissions, or contrary interpretation of the subject matter herein. Any perceived slights of specific persons, peoples, or organizations are unintentional.

Dedication

**My four amazing children,
Whitney, Brooke, Bryce, and Brock,
and their father, Robert (Buzz) Wilson**

They were all willing to try anything that I prepared – experiments, and all. There were more than a few times that we tossed the dinner in the trash and opted for our family default dinner, pancakes and scrambled eggs.

It is also dedicated to my dear mother-in-law, Charlotte. She introduced me to the wonderful world of creative cooking. It was because of her encouragement that I was able to develop the confidence to test my cooking wings!

Thank You

... for buying my book.
If you enjoy it, please take a minute and post
a review on Amazon
Sauce Recipes – 50 Tasty Choices

For a complete list of my published books,
please, visit my Website:

www.mamalegacycookbooks.com

Nancy N. Wilson

Please help me continuously improve my books.
If you find errors or omissions, or have a problem with a recipe,
please, contact me immediately at: wilsonemarketing@gmail.com,
so that I can make the necessary corrections.

Other Books by this Author

Cookbooks

Candy Making Made Easy
Instructions and 17 Starter Recipes

Cake Making Made Easy
Instructions and 60 Cakes

Mama's Legacy Series

Seven Volumes Available
Dinner – 55 Easy Recipes (Volume I)
Breakfast and Brunch – 60 Delicious Recipes (Volume II)
Dessert – 50 Scrumptious Choices (Volume III)
Chicken – 25 Classic Dinners (Volume IV)
Mexican Favorites – 21 Traditional Recipes (Volume V)
Side Dish Recipes (Volume VI)
Sauce Recipes – 50 Tasty Choices (Volume VII)

Health and Fitness

DETOX – The Master Cleanse Diet

Business

Attitude Adjustment

Table of Contents

Introduction

Dear Friends,

Welcome to *Sauce Recipes – 50 Tasty Choices, Volume VII* of *Mama's Legacy Cookbook Series.*

This series was created in honor of all the wonderful women in my life who not only taught me *how* to cook, but also shared with me their *love of cooking.*

Writing cookbooks has been a long-held dream of mine. I have a great passion for well-prepared, delicious food, and hopefully this series will inspire you to stretch your creative cooking wings and begin to build your own collection of recipes that can be shared with others.

I have been collecting recipes for over 60 years. The sources are numerous – beginning with my mother, then friends, colleagues, church groups, and a few updated versions of my own recipes from the Internet. Other origins include old cookbooks going back to my early married years, recipes found in product packaging, and magazines that I have kept in a box in my pantry for eons.

Many were copied exactly from the paper on which they were originally written; some have morphed a little over the years; and some are newer versions of long-held recipes that have been passed from friend to friend to friend.

Sauce Recipes – 50 Tasty Choices, is a special collection of recipes that was created to accompany all the other cookbooks. Often all you need to make a good meal or dessert great is the perfect sauce.

The 50 recipes in this cookbook provide a wide variety of choices in several different categories: sauces for grilling or roasting meat, sweet dessert sauces, essential classic sauces that every cook should know how to make, specialty sauces that are unique and do not fit into the other categories, and sauces for meats and vegetables. And finally, what would a sauce cookbook be without sauce recipes for pasta?

Most of the sauces are fairly quick and easy to prepare, with the exception of a few that take a little more time and effort (but are so worth it) such as: hot caramel, hot fudge, Sharon's Lasagna Sauce and Hollandaise Sauce.

I encourage you to try each one and find your favorites – first for your family and then, others that are perfect for entertaining. Play with the recipes. Almost every sauce recipe can be used in a variety of ways – be creative and have a good time with them.

A good friend of mine once said to me that there are three great pleasures in life: Laughter – Making Love – Great Food. I agreed when he said it, and I still agree all these many years later.

What are your three greatest pleasures? I hope that great food is one of them and that you will find pleasure in using the recipes in this book as much as I found in compiling them for you.

All the best,

Nancy N. Wilson

P. S. I would love to hear about your cooking adventures. Please send me stories. Your personal favorite recipes are also welcome, if you feel like sharing. If I use them in future cookbooks, I will give you credit. You can contact me at wilsonemarketing@gmail.com.

Barbecue
Basting
Marinades
Glazes

Apricot Ham Glaze

Ingredients

1 cup apricot nectar

2/3 cup orange juice

2 tablespoons cornstarch

½ cup apricot preserves

4 pounds whole cooked ham

Directions

Place apricot nectar, orange juice and cornstarch in a small saucepan over medium heat.

Cook until mixture thickens and becomes glossy - stir constantly.

Stir in the apricot preserves and cook until melted well into the mixture.

Place the ham in lightly-greased baking pan and cover with ¼ of the glaze.

Bake the ham according to package directions and baste several times with glaze.

When ham reaches the required temperature *(always use a meat thermometer)*, slice and serve.

Drizzle slices with remaining glaze.

Servings: 8

Chimichurri Sauce

This spicy sauce is an excellent marinade for meats that are to be grilled. It can also be used as a sauce for steak, a good sausage, and fish tacos.

Ingredients

6 cloves garlic, peeled and cut into chunks

1 whole bay leaf

2 whole Jalapeno chilies, coarsely chopped with seeds

1½ tablespoons salt

1 tablespoon Ancho powder

½ cup fresh cilantro, minced

½ cup fresh flat-leaf parsley, minced

¼ cup fresh oregano

¼ cup red wine vinegar

½ cup extra-virgin olive oil

Directions

Trim and peel the garlic and jalapenos *(see tips).*

In a blender puree the following ingredients to a paste: garlic cloves, bay leaf, jalapeno chilies, salt and 1 tablespoon of the vinegar until the paste is formed.

Place the puree in a small bowl and stir in the herbs. *(See tips for substituting dried herbs for fresh herbs.)*

Whisk the remaining vinegar and olive oil together until smooth and add to the puree.

Let the sauce marinate for a few hours before serving as a sauce.

If using as a marinade, marinate the meat for at least three to four hours, turning occasionally.

Servings: 4

Recipe Tips

HERBS:

As a rule of thumb, you can substitute one teaspoon of dried herbs for one tablespoon of fresh herbs and vice-versa (which is a one-to-three ratio). You will learn by taste the exact substitution amounts that you prefer.

Fresh dried herbs have a stronger taste than fresh herbs, but lose their pungency as they age. If your dried herbs have been recently purchased, use a light hand. If you have had them for a while, you will probably need more.

ALWAYS use fresh ingredients if available to ensure the best possible flavor.

CHILIES

Ancho chili powder, made from Ancho (Pablano) peppers, has a rich dark smoky flavor with mild to medium heat.

This pepper is the most commonly used in authentic Mexican cooking and is a staple in red chili and tamales.

It is an excellent choice for a milder chili taste. Use Ancho powder just as you would salt or pepper.

Sprinkle on pasta, baked potatoes, vegetables, soups, pizza, popcorn and more.

Also try it to season chicken, stews, potatoes, vegetables and, of course, Mexican dishes.

NOTE: *Hot peppers contain oils that can burn your skin, lips, and eyes.* Always wear protective gloves or plastic bags on your hands when handling the chilies. Avoid touching your face or eyes when working with the chilies. AND - don't forget to wash your hands thoroughly with hot soapy water when you are finished.

Citrus Chili Barbecue Sauce

A spicy (hot, medium, or mild) Southwestern style citrus barbecue sauce that goes well with beef, pork, poultry, and seafood.

Ingredients

1 large onion, finely chopped

1 tablespoon ground red chilies

¼ teaspoon ground red pepper

1 whole Ancho chili, seeded and finely chopped

1 tablespoon olive oil

1 cup orange juice

½ cup lime juice

2 tablespoons sugar (add to taste)

2 tablespoons lemon juice

1 tablespoon fresh cilantro, finely chopped

1 teaspoon salt

Directions

Heat oil in medium skillet or saucepan.

Add onion, ground red chilies, red pepper powder, and chopped Ancho chili.

Cook until onion is tender, stirring frequently ~ 5 minutes.

Add remaining ingredients and bring to a boil.

Reduce heat to low immediately and simmer uncovered for about 10 minutes - stir occasionally.

Serve immediately.

Yield: 2 1/3 cup (6 servings)

Recipe Tips

NOTE: *Hot peppers contain oils that can burn your skin, lips and eyes.* Always wear protective gloves or plastic bags on your hands when handling them. Avoid touching your face and eyes while working. AND - don't forget to thoroughly wash your hands with hot soapy water when you are finished.

Add more or less Ancho chilies to increase or decrease the heat!

Lemon and Soy Basting Sauce

This quick and easy Asian-flavored basting sauce is excellent for fish or poultry. It should be added during the last 15 minutes of broiling or grilling.

Ingredients

1 tablespoon brown sugar

1 teaspoon cornstarch

2 tablespoons lemon juice

2 tablespoons soy sauce

2 tablespoons water

2 tablespoons green onions (including tips), sliced

1 tablespoon butter

1 clove garlic, minced

Directions

Mix brown sugar and cornstarch together in a saucepan.

Stir in lemon juice, soy sauce and water and heat over medium heat.

Stir in the onion, butter and garlic.

Continue to cook stirring constantly, until thickened and bubbly.

Servings: 6

Recipe Tips

Be careful not to overcook the fish or it will be tough and dried out. This is the single biggest mistake people make when preparing fish.

Louisiana Barbecue Sauce

This New Orleans-style barbecue sauce is absolutely wonderful on ribs, chicken, or pork chops. Be sure to fix a generous amount. The barbecued pieces will disappear quickly.

Ingredients

1/3 cup bourbon or whiskey

1 teaspoon cornstarch

2/3 cup orange juice

1 tablespoon grated orange rind

3 tablespoons molasses

1 cup Basic Barbecue Sauce (see below)

Basic Barbecue Sauce

1 can (8 ounces) tomato sauce

3 tablespoons Worcestershire Sauce

½ cup olive oil

¼ cup cider vinegar

3 teaspoons dry mustard (do not use prepared mustard)

3 tablespoons brown sugar (packed)

2 teaspoons chili powder

2 teaspoon sugar

½ teaspoon garlic powder

2 tablespoons dried minced onion

½ teaspoon salt

¼ teaspoon black pepper

Directions

Basic Barbecue Sauce:
Combine all ingredients and let stand for at least 10 minutes.

Louisiana Barbecue Sauce:
Stir the bourbon (whiskey) into the cornstarch in a small bowl, mix until smooth.

Place all remaining ingredients *(including 1 cup of the basic barbecue sauce)* in a medium-small sauce pan and mix thoroughly.

Cook over medium heat, stirring continuously, until sauce boils.

Reduce heat and simmer 10 minutes.

Ready to use on ribs, chicken or pork chops.

Servings: 6

Pork Basting Sauce

Ingredients

1 tablespoon honey

1 tablespoon Dijon mustard

1 tablespoon soy sauce

1 large clove garlic, peeled and minced

Directions

Stir all ingredients together in a small bowl.

Let sauce stand for at least 10 minutes so flavors can blend.

Grill pork chops over medium-high heat. Turn and baste frequently with sauce - cook for approximately 8 to 10 minutes - until done through.

If cooking pork tenderloin - grill over medium-high heat.

Turn and baste frequently for 30 to 35 minutes - until internal temperature reaches 160 degrees F. *(A meat thermometer is recommended.)*

Servings: 2

Salmon Marinade

Salmon is delicious any time, but when marinated and grilled with this Japanese-style marinade, it is exceptional. Do not overcook.

Ingredients

¼ cup white wine

2 tablespoons lemon juice

¼ cup soy sauce (If you use low sodium, you will have to add a little salt)

1 tablespoon brown sugar

½ teaspoon ginger

Directions

Mix all ingredients together.

In a glass baking dish, place 1½ pounds of salmon that has been cut in the serving sizes that you prefer.

Cover with marinade.

Marinate overnight, turning the salmon two or three times.

Grill and serve hot with Grilled Pineapple, Steamed Green Beans and Rice Pilaf (Recipes can be found in *Side Dishes, Volume VI, Mama's Legacy Cookbook Series).*

Steak Marinade

This is a great marinade that can be used with any steak - excellent for outdoor or indoor grilling.

Ingredients

1 teaspoon lemon peel, grated

½ cup lemon juice

1/3 cup olive oil

2 tablespoons green onions, with tops, peeled and sliced

1 clove garlic, minced

4 teaspoons sugar

1½ teaspoon salt

1 teaspoon Worcestershire Sauce

1 teaspoon prepared mustard

1/8 teaspoon freshly-ground black pepper

Directions

Combine all the marinade ingredients. Pour over steaks.

Marinate 3-4 hours or overnight in the refrigerator, turning steaks several times.

Broil steaks to the degree of doneness you prefer.

Servings: 4

Dessert Sauces

Bourbon Sauce for Bread Pudding
(New Orleans Favorite)

This was a new discovery when I first worked in New Orleans. It was great when I finally found the recipe. For an extra touch of sweetness, add a dollop of hard sauce or sweetened whipped cream.

Ingredients

1 cup sugar

½ cup butter, melted

1 whole egg, lightly beaten

1 tablespoon bourbon (or more – adjust to taste)

½ teaspoon vanilla extract

Directions

Melt butter in a medium-sized saucepan over low heat.

Beat the egg slightly – Whisk in the sugar until well-mixed.

Add egg mixture to melted butter in the sauce pan, whisking continuously to ensure that everything is well-blended.

Continue to cook over the low heat, stirring continuously until mixture thickens.

Remove from heat and stir in vanilla extract and whiskey to taste.

Serve immediately, or let cool and reheat when ready to serve. *(As you reheat the sauce, whisk until it is creamy and smooth.)*

Serve over warm bread pudding (See recipe in *Dessert – 50 Scrumptious Recipes, Volume III, Mama's Legacy Cookbook Series).*

Servings: 8

Crème Anglaise

Crème Anglaise (English Cream) is the French translation for custard sauce. There are two types of custard; cooked (stirred) and baked over water. This is a 'cooked' or 'stirred' custard sauce. The end result is a rich and smooth textured sauce that can be served, warm or cold, with cakes, pies, puddings, or fruit. It is the custard recommended for Ile Flotante (Floating Island) that can be found in <u>Dessert – 50 Scrumptious Recipes, Volume III, Mama's Legacy Cookbook Series</u>.)

Ingredients

2 1/3 cups whole milk (light cream or half-and-half can be used for richer custard)

1 whole vanilla bean, split lengthwise (can be found in specialty food stores) or use 2 teaspoons pure vanilla extract

4 to 5 tablespoons sugar (add more or less to taste)

6 large egg yolks

Directions

Have a fine medium-sized strainer and bowl ready near the stove.

Slice the vanilla bean lengthwise.

Using a wooden spoon and a glass or stainless steel mixing bowl, mix the sugar and yolks gently until well blended, but not frothy. *(Use mixture as quickly as possible – do not let it sit.)*

Heat the milk (cream) with the vanilla bean in a saucepan - bring to a boil and immediately remove from heat. *(After removing from the heat, you can let the milk sit for 15 minutes, which will allow the vanilla to infuse more into the milk. Be sure to remove the skin that will form on the top of the milk.)*

Vigorously whisk in a few tablespoons of the hot milk into the yolk mixture. Then, gradually add the remaining milk to the egg yolk mixture - whisking constantly.

Pour the mixture into a medium-sized saucepan – stir constantly as you gently heat the mixture over medium heat - until just below the boiling point (170° F).

Steam will begin to appear and the mixture will be slightly thicker than heavy cream. DO NOT BOIL or the mixture will curdle.

Check to see if the custard is the right consistency by holding a wooden spoon sideways that is covered with the custard. Run your finger along the back of the spoon. If the streak remains without the cream running down through the streak, it is ready.

Immediately remove from the heat and pour through the strainer, scraping up any thickened cream that settles on the bottom of the pan.

Remove the vanilla bean and scrape the seeds into the sauce. Stir until seeds separate and mix evenly in the sauce. *(If you are using pure vanilla extract, instead of the vanilla bean, add it to the cream now.)*

Yield: 2 ½ to 3 cups (6 to 8 servings)

Recipe Tips

If sauce was overheated and cream begins to separate (curdling), remove from heat and whisk vigorously to smooth out - then return to heat. If necessary, add a little heavy cream to the mixture before blending.

Five-Minute Vanilla Sauce

Serve vanilla sauce warm with apple pie, strudel, apple crisp, bread pudding, and other desserts. It is very versatile. There are more complicated versions of this recipe, but this one is quick and easy.

Ingredients

1 cup water

½ cup sugar

1 tablespoon cornstarch

2 tablespoons butter

2 teaspoons vanilla extract

1 pinch of salt

Directions

Thoroughly mix sugar and cornstarch together in a small bowl.

Bring water to a boil in a small saucepan and slowly stir in the sugar/cornstarch mixture to the boiling water.

Reduce heat to medium and cook until thickened, stirring constantly.

Remove pan from heat and add the butter, vanilla, and salt.

Continue to stir until the butter is melted.

Spoon warm sauce over dessert - apple pie, apple crisp, etc.

Yield: ¾ cup (4 servings)

Recipe Tips

To spice it up a little, add: ¼ teaspoon nutmeg and 1/8 teaspoon allspice.

Hard Sauce

Plum Pudding is a traditional holiday treat that should never be served without Hard Sauce. Since the sauce is so incredibly easy to make, you should try it with other types of desserts, as well - such as bread pudding and gingerbread.

Ingredients

½ cup soft butter

1½ cup powdered sugar

1 teaspoon vanilla or rum extract (or 2 teaspoon of rum or brandy liquor)

Directions

Cream butter with an electric hand mixer on low speed until it looks like whipped cream.

Add ½ of the confectioners' sugar, continuing to beat until mixture is smooth.

Add remaining sugar a little at a time until the sauce is the consistency of smooth peanut butter. You can add up a full 2 cups of sugar, if you prefer to make a slightly larger amount.

Stir in flavoring (vanilla extract, rum or brandy).

The sauce should look and feel much the same as whipped cream cheese.

To thin the sauce, use light cream – adding only a few drops at a time.

You want the sauce to be soft, but firm enough so that you can spoon it by the tablespoon and it will hold together nicely without running or dripping off the spoon.

Serve as dollops on individual servings; or, place on top of a warm plum pudding or warm bread pudding so the sauce will melt and dribble down the sides before slicing to serve.

Servings: 8

Recipe Tips

VARIATIONS:

Add 2 tablespoons of brandy, Cointreau, Grand Marnier.

Plum pudding should be served in small slices because it is very rich.

This sauce will keep up to a week in the refrigerator, so for the holidays, you can make it ahead.

Hot Caramel Sauce

Caramel sauce has always been my first choice for topping on ice cream and this one is amazing! It is easier than you may think, but be sure to take care while cooking - no children in the area. Just let them enjoy the tasty sweetness of the finished product.

Ingredients

1 cup sugar

½ cup water

6 tablespoons butter (do not use margarine)

½ cup heavy whipping cream

Directions

Be sure there are no children in the cooking area - and that they will not suddenly appear while you are cooking. This is a safety issue!

To protect your hands from bubbling sauce, you may want to wear oven mitts. Boiling sugar is much hotter than boiling water.

All ingredients must be in place (in the order you need to use them) - readily accessible while cooking.

The process of making caramel sauce moves quickly and you cannot stop to look for ingredients.

If you do not work fast, the sugar will burn and ruin the sauce; but, if you are prepared and pay attention, the result will be a great hot caramel sauce.

So let's have some fun and begin . . .

Place sugar and water in a very heavy-bottomed 3-quart cooking pot over high-heat. *(NOTE: This recipe works best if a heavy-bottomed pan is used!)*

Stir continuously and vigorously with a whisk or wooden spoon as the sugar begins to melt. Stop stirring immediately as soon as the sugar comes to a boil. You can swirl the pan from this point on.

As soon as all of the sugar crystals have melted and boiled down a little, the liquid sugar will turn dark amber in color.

As soon as the color is right, immediately add the butter to the pan and whisk until the butter is completely melted.

Remove the pan from the heat. Count to three; then, slowly add the cream to the pan, whisking continuously to blend well.

NOTE: When adding butter and cream, the mixture will foam up quite a bit. This is the reason that you must use a 3-quart pan.

Continue to whisk until caramel sauce is smooth.

Let cool in the pan for a few minutes, then pour into a glass mason jar *(any other glass jar will break)* and cool to room temperature. *(Be sure to use pot holders when handling the jar filled with hot caramel sauce - or you will be badly burned, possibly drop the jar, and create an incredible mess!)*

Serve immediately - or store in the refrigerator for up to two weeks.

Sauce should be served warm.

Yield: Makes a little over one cup of sauce (~4 servings)

Recipe Tips

CAUTION: *Be extra careful while you are cooking the sugar.* Once the sugar has melted it has a much higher temperature than boiling water. Also, when you add the cream, the mixture will foam up, so use a pan with high sides.

The sauce is also wonderful for dribbling over whipped cream for homemade lattes - or as topping on warm apple pie a la mode.

Hot Fudge Sauce – The Real Deal!

This is a deep, dark bittersweet hot fudge sauce that becomes slightly firm and chewy when served over ice cream. Classic with vanilla ice cream, but also delicious on peppermint, coffee, strawberry, and chocolate ice cream.

Ingredients

½ cup sugar

¼ cup unsweetened cocoa powder

¼ teaspoon salt

½ cup water

1 cup heavy cream

1 cup light corn syrup

¼ teaspoon distilled white vinegar

4 ounces semisweet or bittersweet chocolate (2 ounces coarsely chopped and 2 ounces finely chopped)

¼ cup unsalted butter (½ cube)

1 tablespoon vanilla extract

Directions

Combine sugar, cocoa, and salt in heavy saucepan.

Working over medium-high heat, stir in ½ cup water and whisk until well blended.

Bring mixture to a simmer.

Remove from heat and whisk in the cream, corn syrup, vinegar, and 2 ounces of the chocolate (coarsely chopped).

Return to medium-high heat and bring to a boil, whisk frequently.

Continue to boil and stirring frequently until the bubbles become small and the syrup is thick and sticky (approximately 5 to 8 minutes) - test with a candy thermometer - should be about 225° F.

Remove from heat and add 2 ounces chocolate (finely chopped), butter, and vanilla.

Whisk until smooth.

Serve at once, or let cool, cover and refrigerate for up to 2 weeks.

Reheat in microwave on half-power of on the stove top over low heat.

Yield: 2½ cups (8 servings)

Recipe Tips

Prepare in advance. Sauce can be quickly reheated in the microwave. Heat for 15 to 30 seconds and stir until it is shiny and smooth again.

Substitute vanilla extract with other flavorings: Rum or brandy extract or 2 tablespoons rum *(alcohol evaporates, so you have to use more liquor that extract).*

Mocha Sauce

This dark mocha sauce is the perfect topping for chocolate mousse.

Ingredients

2/3 cup espresso or very strong coffee

3 tablespoons sugar

8 ounces semisweet or bittersweet chocolate, finely chopped.

2 tablespoons unsalted butter, softened

Directions

Cook the coffee and sugar over very low heat, stirring constantly, until sugar is completely dissolved and the mixture is steaming hot.

Stir in the chocolate and whisk until melted and the sauce is smooth.

Remove from heat and stir in the softened butter, continue to stir until completely mixed and smooth.

Serve at once.

Or, cool to room temperature, cover, and refrigerate for up to two weeks.

Reheat over low heat. If the sauce becomes oily, add a little water.

Servings: 4

Yield: 1½ Cups

Quick Chocolate Mint Sauce

This unusual chocolate sauce will be a real treat for ice cream lovers.

Ingredients

1 bag (13 ounces) chocolate peppermint cream candies

1/3 cup heavy cream

Directions

Chop the peppermint cream patties into small pieces and place in a double boiler over boiling water.

Add the heavy cream and stir until smooth.

Serve warm over ice cream.

Yield: 1½ Cups (4 servings)

Yummy Homemade Chocolate Sauce

You will want to try this one right away! It is so rich and delicious that you will never buy it at the grocery store again. It only takes 10 minutes using ingredients that are always in your pantry, so you can always whip it up when you have that undeniable craving for chocolate.

Ingredients

2¼ cups sugar

¾ cup unsweetened cocoa powder

1½ tablespoons flour

¼ teaspoon salt

1½ cups whole milk

1 tablespoon vanilla extract

Directions

Place sugar, cocoa, flour, and salt in a medium-sized saucepan.

Add ½ cup of the milk and whisk into a thick paste.

Heat over medium heat, stirring constantly.

Stir in the remaining milk, whisking to mix well, and bring mixture to a boil.

As soon as the sauce boils, reduce heat to low and simmer for 5 minutes, stirring often.

Remove from heat, add vanilla extract and let it cool.

Use immediately, or cover and store in the refrigerator for up to two weeks.

Servings: 18

Yield: About 3 cups (18 servings)

VARIATIONS:

This basic sauce is absolutely wonderful and you will want to use it often - as it is! BUT - it can be varied in a number of delicious ways!

1. ***Chocolate Orange Sauce:*** Add orange liqueur and a little orange zest.

2. ***Cherry Bounce Sauce:*** Add 2 tablespoons of bourbon and a few cherries.

3. ***Chocolate Mint Sauce:*** Add a couple of drops of mint extract and chopped fresh mint leaves - (Be careful with the mint, it is very strong).

4. ***Chocolate Peppermint Sauce:*** Add some crushed peppermint candy.

Topping can be used hot or cold; on ice cream, cake, or fruit.

Mix with milk to make a cup of hot (or cold) chocolate (Make it as heavy with chocolate as you like.)

Slice bananas, sprinkle with chopped walnuts and drizzle the chocolate sauce, and the result is an elegant and satisfying dessert.

Since a little bit goes a long way, use it as a low-fat treat - a bite here.....a bite there.

If you are seriously watching fat intake, the sauce can be made with low fat or even skim milk, for a wonderful treat. It is not quite as good as it is when made with whole milk, but for a compromise, it is almost as good and will satisfy your sweet tooth, I promise.

Essential
Sauces

Basic White Sauce

White sauce, also known as Béchamel, is used in a variety of dishes and is the base for many sauces. Here are the steps for a basic medium white sauce, with adjustments for thickness. It is the perfect base for chicken casserole dishes and the wonderful comfort food, macaroni and cheese (my granddaughter's favorite.)

Ingredients

4 tablespoons butter

4 tablespoons flour

2 cups milk

¼ teaspoon salt

1 dash white pepper

1 dash grated or ground nutmeg

Directions

Melt butter in heavy saucepan over medium-low heat.

Stir in flour with a wire whisk – continue whisking until well-blended and smooth.

Cook over low heat for 3 minutes, stirring continuously. Do not allow the mixture to brown. *(This mixture is called a <u>roux</u>.)*

Remove the pan from the heat and whisk in the milk.

Return pan to heat and bring to a simmer, stirring continuously.

Continue cooking and whisking until sauce is very smooth and thickened – approximately 2 to 3 minutes.

Add the dash of nutmeg and season to taste with salt and pepper.

Yield: 2 cups

Recipe Tips

For smaller amount - simply cut the recipe in half.

This basic white sauce can be used in many main dishes. Typically made with milk only, it can be made with half milk and half chicken stock for use in chicken casseroles such as *Chicken Divan*.

For thin white sauce, follow the instructions above, but use 1 tablespoon butter and 1 tablespoon flour. *(Thin white sauce is used in cream soups.)*

For thick white sauce, follow the instructions above, but use 3 tablespoons butter and 3 tablespoons flour. *(Thick white sauce is used in soufflés.)*

For heavy white sauce, follow the instructions above, but use 4 tablespoons of butter and 4 tablespoons flour. *(Heavy white sauce is used as a binder for croquettes.)*

Light stock, cream, or a combination may be used in place of the milk.

Vary the flavor by seasoning with celery salt; a teaspoon of lemon juice, onion juice, or sherry; ½ teaspoon Worcestershire Sauce; or 2 tablespoons chopped chives or parsley.

VARIATIONS:

Veloute Sauce:
Use chicken broth or fish stock instead of milk.

Mornay Sauce:
Add ½ cup of grated Swiss, Gruyere or Emmanthal cheese after sauce thickens. Remove from heat and whisk until melted and smooth.

Onion White Sauce:
Cook 1 tablespoon minced onion in the butter until translucent. Then add the flour and continue with the recipe.

Mustard White Sauce:
Whisk in 1-2 teaspoons prepared mustard after the sauce is thickened.

Brown Sauce:

When cooking the flour and butter mixture together, stir constantly and cook until the mixture begins to turn brown. Use chicken or beef stock instead of the milk.

Curry Sauce:

Add 1-3 teaspoons of curry powder (to taste) to the butter and simmer for 1 minute before adding the flour. Continue with the recipe as directed.

Béarnaise Sauce

Béarnaise Sauce is a classic variation of Hollandaise Sauce that is flavored with tarragon. It is an excellent sauce for roasted meats, potatoes, and fish.

Ingredients

½ cup white wine (or sherry for a nutty flavor)

1 tablespoon shallots (or scallions), finely chopped

½ teaspoon fresh tarragon, chopped (vary amount to personal taste)

3 or 4 large egg yolks

½ teaspoon salt

½ cup butter (do not use margarine)

Directions

Place wine, finely chopped shallots, and chopped tarragon in small sauce pan.

Simmer until wine is cooked down to a glaze.

Blend egg yolks and salt in electric blender.

With blender on low, slowly pour glaze into the egg mixer.

Melt butter to bubbling hot.

Turn blender on low again and pour the bubbling hot butter in a steady stream into the egg mixture - continuously blending.

Continue to blend until mixture thickens.

Serve immediately (see Tips Section).

Servings: 4

Recipe Tips

The sauce should be eaten right away. You can keep it for 30 minutes by putting the sauce in a bowl and placing the bowl in a saucepan or bowl of very hot water.

Béchamel Sauce

Béchamel sauce, more commonly known as white sauce, is one of the mother sauces of French Cuisine and is also used in Italian cuisine, such as Salmon Lasagna. This recipe is slightly more elegant that the <u>Basic White Sauce</u> *recipe above and good to have in your repertoire.*

Ingredients

½ medium onion

2 whole cloves

2½ cups milk

3 tablespoon butter

1/3 cup flour

Salt and pepper to taste

1 pinch nutmeg (freshly grated is preferred)

Directions

Peel the onion and place two cloves into the onion.

Place the onion (with the cloves) and the bay leaf into the milk in a small sauce pan over low heat.

Simmer for 15 minutes.

Remove from the heat and discard the seasonings, set seasoned milk aside.

In another small sauce pan, melt the butter over medium heat.

When butter is melted, reduce the heat to low and add the flour. Mix thoroughly with wooden spoon.

Cook over low heat for 2 or 3 minutes, stirring frequently.

Remove from heat and gradually whisk in the seasoned milk.

Return the mixture to the low heat and bring to a simmer, whisking constantly.

Continue to cook, stirring gently for 7 to 10 minutes until thickened.

Season with salt, pepper, and nutmeg.

The sauce is ready to serve.

To store: place a plastic wrap directly on top of the sauce to prevent a skin from forming on the surface.

Yield: 2½ Cups

Recipe Tips

VARITIONS: See "Tips" under <u>Basic</u> White Sauce recipe above.

Beurre Blanc

Beurre Blanc translated from French mean "white butter." This buttery, spicy sauce is excellent with seared ahi tuna, steamed or poached salmon, sea bass, or fillet of sole.

Ingredients

1 whole shallot, trimmed and peeled

½ cup cold butter (1 cube)

7 tablespoons dry white wine (Muscadet is a good choice ~ 2 small glasses)

3 tablespoons white wine vinegar

Salt and pepper to taste

Directions

Trim, peel and finely chopped the shallot.

Cut the butter into little pieces.

In a small saucepan over low heat - heat the wine, vinegar and shallot.

Season with salt and pepper.

Cook the mixture down to approximately ¾ of original amount and remove from heat.

Strain the reduced liquid and return it to the pan - discard the shallot.

Gradually whisk in the pieces of butter - they should soften nicely - return to very low heat is needed to soften (not melt) the butter.

Check the seasoning and adjust as needed.

Serve immediately.

Yield: 1 Cup (6 to 8 servings)

Blue Cheese Sauce

This incredibly delicious sauce can be made in five minutes and will dramatically enhance grilled or fried steak and potatoes.

Ingredients

3½ ounces blue cheese (you can combine several types of blue cheese, such as Roquefort, Gorgonzola, Bresse Bleu)

2/3 cup sour cream (or crème fraîche)

¼ cup Greek-style plain yogurt (optional)

Directions

Place the sour cream (crème fraîche) and cheese in a small saucepan over a low heat.

Stir to let the cheese melt slowly, then increase the heat and bring the mixture to a boil, stirring constantly with a wooden spoon.

Remove from the heat as soon as the sauce adheres to the wooden spoon.

Add the yogurt for a lighter sauce with a touch of acidity.

Season to taste with salt and pepper – be careful with the salt since the cheese is already salty.

Yield: 1 cup

Recipe Tips

Crème fraîche literally means 'fresh cream' in French. However, it is a sour cream that is made with bacterial culture, but is thinner and less sour than American sour cream and has a higher fat content.

Serving Suggestion:
Coarsely chop a couple of large potatoes and fry in a heavy frying pan with butter until almost tender and lightly browned. Remove the potatoes and keep warm while cooking the steaks.

Fry the steaks in the same pan to your preferred level of doneness, or you can grill the steaks on an outdoor grill while cooking the potatoes inside.

Serve the steaks and fried potatoes with the blue cheese sauce and a little chopped chervil, if desired.

Easy Hollandaise Sauce

You no longer have to be afraid to make Hollandaise Sauce – anyone can make it with this recipe and enjoy the results. Eggs Benedict, anyone? (Recipe in <u>Breakfast and Brunch, Volume II, Mama's Legacy Series</u>)

Ingredients

1 cube unsalted butter (do not use margarine)

3 large egg yolks

1 tablespoon lemon juice

1 tablespoon sherry

3 dashes cayenne pepper

½ teaspoon salt (If using salted butter, omit the salt)

Directions

Melt the butter in a small sauce pan and remove from heat as soon as it is melted. Do not let it sizzle.

Place the egg yolks, lemon juice, sherry, salt and cayenne in an electric blender and blend on medium speed for 20 to 30 seconds or until mixture lightens in color.

When color changes, reduce the speed to lowest setting and very slowly add the melted butter. Continue to blend for 3 or 4 seconds after all the butter has been added.

Taste the sauce – it should taste buttery, lemony, and very lightly salted. If necessary, add the necessary ingredients (salt or lemon) to enhance the flavor.

If you want the sauce thinner, add a little warm water and pulse two or three short pulses to thoroughly mix the additional ingredients.

Either serve immediately, or keep the sauce in a warm place (stove top) and serve within an hour.

Servings: 4 to 6

Hollandaise Sauce (The Classic)

This is a classic sauce that is the crowning glory of Eggs Benedict. I also use it in my Chicken Divan recipe (Chicken – 25 Classic Dinners, Volume IV, Mama's Legacy Series). I am sure you will find many other uses for it, as well. There is an "easy" version included this cookbook, just before this recipe; but, I prefer the original. Hollandaise can also be served with asparagus, artichokes and new potatoes.

Ingredients

3 tablespoons butter

½ teaspoon cornstarch

¼ teaspoon salt

3 large egg yolks

2 tablespoons lemon juice

½ cup boiling water

Directions

Cream butter, cornstarch, and salt together. Place in double boiler over warm (not boiling) water.

Using a wooden spoon, add egg yolks to mixture, one at a time.

Blend lemon juice and water and stir into mixture, stirring continuously.

When the water in the bottom of the double boiler starts to boil, cook 5 to 8 minutes.

Cook until soft custard consistency.

Season to taste with salt and pepper.

The sauce should be served immediately.

Recipe Tips

Follow directions carefully to avoid curdling.

Quick Brown Sauce

Serve as you would brown gravy with meats or other dishes. The sauce can also be used as base for Bordelaise sauce.

Ingredients

½ large clove garlic, peeled

3 tablespoons butter

3 tablespoons flour

1½ cups beef consommé

½ teaspoon thyme (or another herb of your choice)

1 sprig fresh parsley

Salt and freshly ground-pepper

Directions

Peel and cut a clove of garlic.

Rub a medium-sized, heavy sauce pan with the garlic, covering the sides and bottom of the pan well.

Melt the butter over medium heat and stir in the flour; continue to stir until blended.

Continue to cook and stir until mixture is lightly browned and has a nutty smell, approximately 7 minutes.

Heat bouillon or stock in the microwave.

Slowly stir into the roux *(flour and butter mixture).*

Bring to a boil, whisking constantly until sauce begins to thicken.

Add herbs, reduce heat and simmer for a few more minutes until sauce is thickened.

Adjust seasoning with salt and freshly-ground black pepper to taste.

For variations of flavor, season to taste with one of the following:

- Paprika
- Fresh lemon juice
- Dry sherry
- Worcestershire Sauce
- Combination of different herbs

Yield: 1 cup (4 servings)

Gravies

Au Jus

Au Jus is the final touch with any prime rib roast. Serve with <u>Creamy Horseradish Sauce</u> and all the trimmings.

Ingredients

All the drippings (juice) from a cooked Prime Rib Roast

2 teaspoons Worcestershire Sauce

1 cup beef broth/stock – homemade is best. (If you must use canned, use unsalted or low sodium)

½ cup red wine (your choice – nice to use some of the red wine you will be serving with the meal)

Directions

Skim off all the fat from the drippings in the roasting pan and return 2 tablespoons to the drippings.

Place the roasting pan over two stove top burners on medium-low heat.

Whisk in the Worcestershire Sauce and the broth, gently scrape the bottom of the pan to loosen any browned bits on the bottom pan.

Bring mixture to a boil and simmer for 2 or 3 minutes.

Add red wine of your choice. *(Keep in mind that the Au Jus will only be as good as the broth and wine you choose.)*

Bring to a boil and cook until the liquid is slightly reduced ~ 5 minutes.

Season to taste with salt and pepper.

Serve with your prime rib.

Recipe Tips

Even though I have given you a recipe, making Au Jus is more of a technique than a recipe. Mastering the art requires guess work depending on the following:

> 1 - How much juice is left in your pan, plus the juice from slicing the prime rib roast.
>
> 2 - How many people you will be serving. Adjust your beef broth and/or wine according to how much Au Jus you think you will need for each person being served.

Use any leftover Prime Rib and Au Jus for making French Dip Sandwiches for your family the next day. So good!

Milk Gravy

Creamy milk gravy was a constant in my childhood home and is still my favorite type of gravy. It is perfect with fried chicken and mashed potatoes or as sausage gravy on biscuits for breakfast (Recipe in Breakfast and Brunch, Volume II, Mama's Legacy Series).

Ingredients

¼ pan drippings from fried chicken, bacon, sausage, or meat

¼ cup flour

1 can evaporated milk (regular) - add enough water to make two cups

½ teaspoon salt (adjust to taste)

¼ teaspoon pepper (adjust to taste)

Directions

Remove chicken or meat from the frying pan.

Scrape up excessive crumbs, breading, etc. from the bottom of the pan and remove with a slotted spoon.

Strain the drippings into a glass measuring cup.

Return ¼ cup of the drippings back to the frying pan and heat over medium heat.

Stir in ¼ cup flour into the heated drippings.

Cook and continuously stir the drippings and flour mixture until mixture starts to bubble and browns nicely - usually about 5 minutes, but could possibly take a little more.

Season with salt and pepper to taste.

Slowly add the milk to the frying pan, stirring constantly with wire whisk.

Continue cooking and stirring continuously until gravy comes to a boil and thickens.

If gravy is too thick, add a little milk. If too thin, add a little flour/water mixture until it reaches the thickness you prefer.

Adjust seasonings to taste.

Yield: 2 cups (4 Servings)

Recipe Tips

VARIATION:

Easy Potato Casserole:
Cook 3 or 4 large potatoes until almost done. Cool slightly, peel, and slice. Layer the potatoes with sautéed onions, grated cheese and the milk gravy. Bake at 350° until heated through and bubbly.

This variation comes from one of my reviewers. Couldn't resist adding it!

Thanksgiving Turkey Gravy

Thanksgiving dinner is one of my family's favorite dinners and the gravy ties it all together. I struggled with gravy for years and then, I found this recipe. I hope your family enjoys it as much as mine does.

Ingredients

1 package neck, heart, gizzard from turkey giblets (discard the liver)

1 medium carrot, peeled and cut into 2" – 3" chunks

1 medium onion, peeled, trimmed, and cut into quarters

1 medium celery stalk, cut into 4 or 5 pieces

½ teaspoon salt

3 tablespoons fat from turkey drippings

3 tablespoons flour

½ teaspoon salt

1/3 cup sherry

Salt and pepper to taste

Directions

Place turkey giblets and salt in a 3-quart saucepan over high heat. Add just enough water to cover the giblets.

Over medium-high heat, bring the giblets to a boil; then, turn heat down to low, cover and simmer for 45 minutes.

Strain giblet broth into a large bowl or covered glass container. Cover and place in the refrigerator.

ROAST THE TURKEY (or Chicken)

Recipe in *Chicken – 25 Classic Dinners, Volume IV, Mama's Legacy Cookbook Series.*

MAKE THE GRAVY

When the turkey is done, remove it from the roasting pan.

Pour all the drippings from the pan through a sieve into a 4-cup measuring cup.

Place the roasting pan back on the stop over medium heat and add 1 cup giblet broth into the pan

Heat and stir until the crusty brown bits on the bottom of the pan are loosened - then, add the mixture to the drippings in the measuring cup.

Let the mixture stand a few minutes, until the fat rises to the top.

Scoop off 3 tablespoons of the fat that has risen to the top and place in a 2-quart saucepan over medium heat.

Add 3 tablespoons of flour and salt into the heated fat. Cook and stir until the mixture is bubbly and golden brown.

Skim and discard any remaining fat on top of the drippings mixture.

Add remaining broth and enough water to the drippings to equal 3½ cups and gradually whisk the liquid into the saucepan with the bubbling, golden brown roux (flour/fat mixture).

Finally, whisk in the sherry to the gravy - continue to cook, stirring occasionally.

Season with salt and pepper and heat to the simmering point - cook until gravy is at the desired thickness.

Serve hot in a warm gravy boat.

Yield: 3¾ cups (15 servings)

Turkey Gravy (Make in Advance)

This delicious gravy can be made in advance, so preparing the meal on Thanksgiving Day is slightly less hectic. The gravy will keep for up to three months when frozen in an airtight container.

Ingredients

6 turkey wings

2 medium onions, peeled and quartered

1 cup water

2 quarts chicken broth, divided

¾ cup chopped carrot

½ teaspoon dried thyme

¾ cup all-purpose flour

2 tablespoons butter

¼ teaspoon ground black pepper

Directions

Preheat oven to 400° F.

Arrange a single layer of turkey wings in a large roasting pan.

Scatter the onions over the top of the wings.

Roast in the preheated oven for 1¼ hours or until wings are browned.

Place browned wings and onions in a 5-quart stockpot.

Add water to roasting pan and stir, scraping up any brown bits on the bottom of the pan.

Pour the water from the pan into the stockpot.

Stir in 6 cups broth, carrot, and thyme - bring to a boil.

Reduce heat to medium-low and simmer uncovered for 1½ hours.

Remove wings from the pot and place on a cutting board.

When the wings are cool, pull off the skin and meat.

Discard the skin and save the meat for another use *(e.g. chicken salad).*

Strain contents of stockpot through a large strainer into a 3 quart saucepan.

Press on the vegetables to extract any remaining liquid.

Discard the vegetables and skim the fat off the liquid.

Bring the contents of the pot to a gentle boil.

In a medium bowl, whisk flour into the remaining 2 cups chicken broth until smooth.

Gradually whisk the flour mixture into the simmering turkey broth; simmer 3-4 minutes or until the gravy has thickened. Stir in the butter and pepper.

Pour into containers and refrigerate or freeze until ready to use. *(Can also be served immediately – and store the leftover gravy for later use.)*

Yield: 8 cups (16 servings)

Specialty Sauces

Caesar Salad Dressing

This dressing is the essential element of a good Caesar Salad (See recipe in Tips Section). And . . . is a delicious choice for any fresh green salad.

Ingredients

1 large clove garlic

2 whole anchovies in oil, very finely chopped

1 whole fresh lemon, juice only

1 large egg yolk

1 dash Worcestershire Sauce

1 teaspoon prepared mustard

2/3 cup extra-virgin olive oil – high grade only

Directions

Peel and crush the garlic.

Finely chop the anchovies.

Juice the lemon.

Place the egg, garlic, anchovies, Worcestershire Sauce, mustard and 1 tablespoon lemon juice in a small bowl.

Whisk together until thoroughly mixed.

Gradually add the oil.

The dressing should be thick, but still runny.

Keep refrigerated in a tightly closed jar until ready for use.

Yield: ¾ Cup

Recipe Tips

Caesar Salad:
Wash and drain 1 head fresh, crisp head romaine lettuce.

Toss salad with the dressing; add a few croutons, and some parmesan shavings.

You can also add sautéed chicken breasts, or slices of avocado sprinkled with lemon juice.

Cocktail Sauce (Shrimp or Crab)

This sauce is excellent as a sauce for shrimp or crab cocktail.

Ingredients

1 cup catsup

1 tablespoon horseradish

1 teaspoon lemon juice

1 teaspoon Worcestershire Sauce

1 dash garlic salt

Few drops Tabasco Sauce to taste

Directions

Mix all ingredients together and chill well, preferably overnight.

Yield: 1 cup

Green Curry (Paste) Sauce

Green Curry is one of the milder curries – heat can be adjusted by using more or less green chilies. This recipe makes an excellent sauce for chicken, beef, or shrimp. Serve with a crisp green salad and steamed jasmine rice. (Recipe in <u>Side Dishes, Volume VI, Mama's Legacy Series</u>.)

Ingredients

½ small bunch fresh cilantro

3 cloves garlic

2 whole shallots

1 piece fresh ginger (thumb-sized piece, peeled and sliced very thin)

4 stalks lemon grass, minced – you can substitute prepared frozen or bottled lemongrass (available at Asian stores)

3 fresh green chilies (adjust to taste)

2 whole fresh limes

1 dash fish sauce

½ teaspoon black peppercorns

1½ cups coconut milk

Directions

Wash and drain the cilantro - cut and discard any hard stems or dead leaves.

Cut off and discard any hard parts of the lemon grass.

Seed the chili peppers. *(Be sure to use protective gloves or plastic bags on your hands - do not touch your face and wash your hands thoroughly when finished with the chilies.)*

Peel the garlic, shallots, and ginger.

Zest 1 lime and squeeze the juice of two limes.

Blend all of the above ingredients until you have a uniform paste.

NOTE: At this point the paste can be used in any recipe that calls for green curry paste.

Heat oil in a large pot - add the curry paste and cook for a few minutes, stirring constantly.

Add the coconut milk and simmer for a few more minutes.

The sauce is ready to use.

Servings: 4

Recipe Tips

Green Curry Chicken

In a wok, large heavy-duty pot or skillet, heat 1½ cups coconut cream over medium heat until boiling. Add green curry sauce and stir well. Continue to boil and add ½ cup (about 120 grams) boneless chicken breast, diagonally sliced, ½" thick and boil for about 10 minutes until chicken is cooked.

Serve hot with jasmine rice and garnish with fresh basil.

Homemade Pizza Sauce

This sauce has great flavor. Be sure to add all the ingredients - it is worth it!

Ingredients

1 can (6 ounces) tomato paste

6 ounces warm water

3 tablespoons Parmesan cheese, grated

1 teaspoon garlic, minced

2 tablespoons honey

1 teaspoon anchovy paste (optional)

¾ teaspoon onion powder

¼ teaspoon dried oregano

¼ teaspoon dried marjoram

¼ teaspoon dried basil

¼ teaspoon ground black pepper

1/8 teaspoon cayenne pepper

1/8 teaspoon dried red pepper flakes

Salt to taste

Directions

In a small bowl combine all the ingredients and mix well, breaking up any clumps of cheese.

Sauce should sit for 30 minutes to blend flavors; spread over pizza dough and prepare pizza as desired.

Yield: 1 pizza (2 servings)

Ranchero Sauce

Many cultures around the globe would recognize Ranchero Sauce. It is often used as a table sauce the way we use catsup or Tabasco. It is a delicious and versatile sauce perfect for making Huevos Rancheros or to top grilled chicken, fish, or sirloin steak, even vegetables; and it is a friend to all beans.

Ingredients

MIX TOGETHER

3 fresh Serrano or Jalapeno chilies, seeded and diced

4 to 6 tablespoons pure ground red chili (or more to taste)

¼ medium onion

2 scallions or green onions

½ stalk celery with some leaves

1 large ripe tomato, squeeze out juice and seeds

3 to 4 large cloves garlic, minced

ADD

1 tablespoon dried oregano

1 teaspoon cumin seed

¼ cup dry red wine

1 large grind of fresh black pepper

1 dash distilled vinegar

1 pinch sugar and salt

1 cup or enough water, wine or good beer for a sauce-like consistency

Directions

Prepare the vegetables as described. *(First seven ingredients)*

Blend together in a food *processor (or chop very finely)* and then place in a saucepan.

Add oregano, cumin, dry red wine, black pepper, vinegar, sugar, salt and enough liquid *(water wine, or good beer)* for a sauce-like consistency.

Simmer Ranchero Sauce gently for about 15 minutes, stir occasionally.

Serve as is, or let the sauce cool and blend it to a puree.

Store in the refrigerator.

Recipe Tips

This sauce keeps well in the refrigerator.

Ranchero Sauce is also well-known as a major ingredient of a Bloody Mary, which many people find worthy to battle the fearsome hangover.

Carne Adovado de Venado:
Soak 2" pieces of meat in the sauce overnight; then, cover and roast slowly at 250° F. for 4-5 hours or until nice and tender.

Traditional Enchilada Sauce

This is very close to the recipe given to me years ago in California by Alicia, who owned a small Mexican restaurant very near our home.

Ingredients

3 tablespoons lard – traditional choice and adds a unique flavor. You can substitute vegetable oil.

1 tablespoon flour

¼ cup chili powder

2 cups chicken stock

1 can (10 ounces) tomato paste

1 teaspoon dried oregano

1 teaspoon ground cumin

½ teaspoon salt

Directions

In medium saucepan heat oil, add flour, smoothing and stirring with a wooden spoon - cook for 1 minute.

Add chili powder and cook for 30 seconds.

Add stock, tomato paste, oregano, and cumin - stir to combine.

Bring to a boil, reduce heat to low, and cook for 15 minutes.

The sauce will thicken and smooth out.

Adjust the seasonings.

Serve on your favorite enchiladas sprinkled with grated cheese and green onions and sides of guacamole and sour cream for toppings.

Yield: 2½ cups (4 servings)

Meat and Vegetable Sauces

Cheese Sauce

This sauce is good with poultry and vegetables. It is perfect for a medley of steamed vegetables, cauliflower and peas, or a single dish such as broccoli.

Ingredients

½ cup butter

3 tablespoons flour

½ tablespoon prepared mustard

1½ cups milk

½ pound grated cheese

½ teaspoon salt

1 dash cayenne pepper

1 dash paprika

1 tablespoon onion juice (or crushed finely chopped onions)

1 tablespoon Worcestershire Sauce

Directions

Blend butter, flour, and mustard together in a saucepan.

Add milk and place over low heat, stirring constantly until heated through.

Add grated cheese and all seasonings.

Mixture will begin to thicken gradually.

When it reaches your desired consistency, remove from the heat.

Serve warm with chicken or on vegetables.

Yield: 1¼ cups (5 servings)

Recipe Tips

VARIATIONS:

Use the sauce with 2 tablespoon chopped pimiento to make *Au Gratin Potatoes (See Side Dish Recipes, Volume VI, Mama's Legacy Series)*

Add ½ cup tomatoes to use for *Shrimp Creole*.

Creamy Horseradish Sauce

Horseradish sauce is a 'must have' for a great prime rib dinner and is also excellent with steak.

Ingredients

> 1 cup whipping cream
>
> ½ cup freshly ground pure horseradish
>
> 1/3 cup mayonnaise (Hellman's or Best Foods are recommended)
>
> 1 teaspoon dry mustard
>
> 1 generous dash cayenne pepper

Directions

Mix all the ingredients together in a small bowl, except the whipping cream.

Whip the cream until stiff peaks form - do not sweeten.

Gently fold in the remaining mixed ingredients.

Serve alongside a Prime Rib Roast cooked to perfection and <u>Au Jus</u> from the drippings.

Servings: 8

Dried Cherry Relish

This tangy combination of ingredients is great with roasted turkey and as a side dish with thick, juicy hamburgers.

Ingredients

½ cup dried cherries

½ cup cherry preserves

2 tablespoons red wine vinegar

½ cup red onion, chopped

¼ whole yellow bell pepper, chopped very fine

¼ whole green bell pepper, chopped very fine

1 tablespoon fresh thyme, finely chopped, or ½ teaspoon dried thyme leaves

Directions

In a small microwave-safe bowl, mix dried cherries, preserves, and vinegar.

Microwave on high 1 to 1½ minutes or until hot through – allow to stand for 5 minutes.

Mix in the onion, peppers, and thyme - stir well.

Cover and refrigerate for a minimum of 3 hours, preferably overnight.

Serve as a sauce with roast turkey, chicken, hamburgers, etc.

Yield: 1½ cups (8 servings)

Lemon Tartar Sauce

Tartar sauce is a delicious condiment for grilled fish, shellfish, and shrimp. It makes a great sandwich spread and is an absolute must for fish and chips.

Ingredients

¾ cup mayonnaise (Best foods or Hellmann's are recommended)

2 tablespoons dill pickle, finely chopped

2 tablespoons green onions, finely chopped

1 tablespoon lemon peel, freshly grated

2 teaspoon lemon juice

Directions

Combine all ingredients in a small bowl, mix thoroughly.

Cover and place in the refrigerator for at least 4 hours, 6+ hours would be better.

Stir two or three times during the refrigeration stage to blend the flavors.

Yield: ¾ cup (6 servings)

Recipe Tips

For a slightly different flavor, add 1½ teaspoons prepared mustard.

Or, add 2 tablespoons catsup and 2 teaspoons Tabasco.

Naturally Sweet Date Sauce

Dates are a fresh, natural whole fruit that provides valuable nutrients and pure sweetness. This is a delicious alternative to the traditional cranberry sauce for the Holidays. Or, if your family loves turkey as much as mine, this is a nice addition to a Sunday family dinner or for guests.

Ingredients

½ pound tiny pearl onions

3 tablespoons butter

¼ cup sugar

3 tablespoons balsamic vinegar

1 cup dry white wine

2 whole cloves

½ teaspoon fresh lemon peel, grated

1½ cups dates, coarsely chopped

1½ cups cranberries, whole

2 teaspoons cornstarch

¼ cup orange juice

Directions

Trim ends from onions and blanch in boiling water for 1 minute, Rinse with cold water and remove skins.

Melt butter in heavy saucepan over medium-high heat and stir in onions until well-coated.

Add sugar, vinegar, wine, cloves and lemon peel and bring to a boil.

Reduce heat to low, cover and cook until onions are soft ~ 35 to 40 minutes. Increase heat to medium-high and add dates and cranberries.

Bring mixture to a boil and cook for 1 to 2 minutes - until cranberries are beginning to burst.

Mix cornstarch and orange juice together until smooth and add to saucepan - cook and stir until mixture thickens.

Serve warm over roast turkey or ham.

OR, cool to room temperature and serve as a condiment.

Servings: 6

Raspberry Sauce (Also for Desserts)

Raspberry sauce adds color and flavor to many dishes. It is amazing with pork tenderloin and grilled chicken breasts. As a dessert, serve it with chocolate cake, poached pears, ice cream, chocolate or lemon mousse, and white chocolate cheesecake.

Ingredients

1 package (10 ounces) frozen raspberries (unsweetened)

¼ cup sugar

2 tablespoons cornstarch

1 to 2 tablespoons orange Liqueur (to taste)

Directions

Place frozen raspberries in a measuring cup and add enough water to make 1½ cups.

Place berries/water combination in a 1-quart sauce pan and stir in sugar and cornstarch.

Bring to a boil, stirring constantly.

Cook and stir for 1 minute and remove from heat.

Strain the sauce, removing all the seeds.

Stir in the liqueur.

Serve with port tenderloin or grilled chicken breasts.

Yield: ~ 1 cup (4 servings)

Tangy Lemon Sauce (Also for Desserts)

This tasty sauce has so many uses. It is great on white fish such as halibut to add a little zing, or on vegetables such as asparagus or broccoli. And . . . changing directions, served warm over cheesecake it is a surprise contrast in hot and cold, zesty and mild.

Ingredients

½ cup sugar

1 tablespoon cornstarch

¼ teaspoon salt

1 cup boiling water

1 tablespoon finely grated lemon peel

2 tablespoons fresh lemon juice

1 tablespoon butter

Directions

Mix sugar, cornstarch and salt in small sauce pan.

Add boiling water and stir vigorously with wire whisk to blend the cornstarch.

Continue to stir and cook until mixture is clear and thick.

Stir in lemon peel, lemon juice, and butter.

Serve warm over fish or steamed vegetables (or both).

Servings: 6

Teriyaki Sauce

Serve with thin slices of beef tenderloin that has been seared in sunflower oil. Pour the sauce over the beef and top with finely chopped green onions.

Ingredients

1/3 cup Sake (Japanese rice wine)

1/3 cup Mirin (sweet, low alcohol content, Japanese cooking wine)

1/3 cup light soy sauce

½ teaspoon sugar

Directions

Place all ingredients in a sauce pan.

Gently bring to a simmer.

Stir to dissolve the sugar.

Cook for 5 to 7 minutes or until the sauce is reduce to a slightly thickened syrup.

The sauce is ready to use.

Zesty Creamy Steak Sauce

So quick - so easy - so good! This smooth, tangy sauce is so pleasing to most taste buds that you will be an instant celebrity chef among your friends. It is perfect with steak, but also good with chicken and shrimp.

Ingredients

1¼ cups mayonnaise (Best Foods or Hellmann's recommended) – do not use low-fat mayo or Miracle Whip.

¼ cup water

1 teaspoon tomato paste (no substitutions – including catsup)

½ teaspoon dry mustard (Do not use prepared mustard)

1 teaspoon vinegar (optional, use if you want a little more zing)

1 tablespoon butter, melted (do not use margarine)

½ teaspoon garlic powder

1 teaspoon sugar

¼ teaspoon paprika

1 dash cayenne pepper (adjust to taste)

Directions

In an electric blender, blend all ingredients until mixture is smooth.

Refrigerate overnight for flavors to blend.

Let sit before serving, best at room temperature.

Servings: 6

Yield: 1½ Cups

Recipe Tips

Use the sauce within 10 days. It will not keep beyond that time.

Hellmann's is called "Best Foods" west of the Rocky Mountains. This is by far the best brand! Use other brands at your own risk. A bad brand can make the sauce taste like mayonnaise rather than a yummy steak sauce.

Pasta
Sauces

Alfredo Sauce

Alfredo Sauce on pasta is a quick, easy, and inexpensive entrée. This recipe has a secret ingredient – cream cheese! It is smooth and delicious. Serve with broccoli and a fresh fruit salad – the result is a lovely family dinner in minutes.

Ingredients

½ cup butter

1 package (8 ounces) cream cheese

2 teaspoon garlic powder

2 cups milk

6 ounces Parmesan cheese, grated

1/8 teaspoon ground black pepper

1 tablespoon fresh parsley, finely chopped (optional)

Fresh parsley for garnish

Directions

Prepare pasta of your choice according to package instructions.

In a non-stick saucepan, melt the butter over medium heat.

Add cream cheese and garlic powder, stirring constantly until smooth - a wire whisk is preferable.

Continue whisk while adding the milk a little at a time, making sure to smooth out any lumps.

Add Parmesan and pepper and continue to cook and stir.

When sauce reaches desired consistency, remove from heat.

Watch the mixture carefully. Once the sauce begins to thicken, it will thicken rapidly.

Thin with milk if you accidentally cook the sauce too long.

Add the finely chopped parsley if you are using it.

Pour over 1 pound pasta of your choice, cooked according to package instructions and toss.

Serve immediately - garnished with fresh parsley sprigs.

Servings: 4

Basil Pesto Sauce

Pesto is good on any type of pasta or even gnocchi and it is perfect for the autumn and winter months. It is wonderful on French bread for an easy, delicious snack and a perfect choice when baking chicken breasts for a quick, easy meal. (See DINNER – 55 Easy Recipes, Volume I, Mama's Legacy Series.)

Ingredients

2 cups fresh basil leaves (loosely packed)

1/3 cup pine nuts

½ cup Parmesan cheese, grated

2 medium cloves garlic, peeled and cut in half

¾ teaspoon salt

½ teaspoon freshly-ground black pepper

1½ teaspoon fresh lemon juice

¼ teaspoon lemon peel, grated

½ cup extra-virgin olive oil

Directions

Place the basil leaves, parmesan cheese, pine nuts and garlic cloves in a food processor or large blender.

Process to a rough paste.

With the machine running on low, slowly add the olive oil - using only as much as needed.

If pesto seems dry (it should be a thick paste), add a little more olive oil.

Season to taste with salt and black pepper.

Serve immediately or pour a very thin film of olive oil over top.

Yield: 1 Cup

Recipe Tips

Pesto must be made with fresh basil, but it can be made in advance.

Pour any pesto you aren't using immediately into an ice cube tray, cover with plastic wrap, and store in freezer for up to three months.

When ready to use, just pop out a couple of cubes from the freezer and add to a pasta dish for a quick and easy meal.

Note: If you plan to make a large batch and freeze it, it is best to add the nuts and cheese after thawing.

VARIATION:

Try using almonds and hazelnuts in place of pints nuts - may need 1 to 2 extra tablespoons of oil when using these nuts.

Best Marinara Sauce

This is a delicious traditional-style red sauce for pasta. For a tasty, quick meal that the young ones will love, prepare the sauce on the weekend when you have time, refrigerate, and then serve with your favorite pasta on a week night when you are too tired to cook.

Ingredients

2 cans (14.5 ounces) stewed tomatoes

1 can (6 ounces) tomato paste

4 tablespoons fresh parsley, finely chopped

1 large clove garlic, minced

1 teaspoon dried oregano

1 teaspoon salt

¼ teaspoon freshly-ground black pepper

6 tablespoons olive oil

1/3 cup onion, finely chopped

½ cup white wine

Directions

In a food processor or large electric blender place Italian tomatoes, tomato paste, chopped parsley, minced garlic, oregano, salt, and pepper. Blend until smooth.

In a large skillet over medium heat sauté the finely chopped onion in olive oil for 2 minutes.

Add the blended tomato sauce and white wine.

Simmer for 30 minutes, stirring occasionally.

Yield: Yield 4 cups (6 servings)

Lemon Cream Sauce

If you want an incredibly quick and tasty meal, start right here. This light lemon cream sauce is delicious on fresh ravioli (spinach, ricotta, or pumpkin) or fresh tagliatelle.

Ingredients

1 whole lemon, zest and juice

3 tablespoons butter (salted)

1 scant cup light cream (half-and-half)

Directions

Zest the lemon completely with the fine side of a grater.

Juice the lemon.

Melt butter in small saucepan over low heat.

Add cream, salt, pepper, lemon zest and lemon juice to the melted butter.

Slowly bring to a boil and simmer for 2 minutes.

Ready to serve.

Yield: 1 Cup

Quick Garlic and Oil Sauce

Aglio e olio (garlic and oil) is the sauce for late-night spaghetti when you find yourself hungry, don't have anything fresh on hand and are too tired to spend a lot of time cooking.

Ingredients

3 cloves garlic (use medium to large cloves)

4 tablespoons extra-virgin olive oil (high-quality)

1 generous pinch red pepper flakes, crushed (adjust to taste)

Salt and pepper to taste

Directions

Peel the garlic and slice it as finely as possible.

Heat oil in sauce pan.

Add garlic and pepper flakes to the hot oil.

Sauté garlic over medium heat until very lightly browned.

If you prefer, you can strain the sauce to remove the pieces of garlic.

The sauce is ready to serve, or you can thin it with a little of the pasta cooking water.

Serve over 7 ounces of spaghetti cooked according to package instructions and well drained.

Serve with hot buttered French bread.

Yield: 3 to 4 tablespoons

Recipe Tips

VARIATION:

For a crispier texture to the sauce, add bread crumbs and chopped flat-leaf parsley that have been lightly browned in oil.

Sharon's Lasagna Sauce

This recipe was given to me by a wonderful sister-in-law when my children were very young. Using it for family dinners and parties has brought many years of delicious delight to all of us. The recipe makes a large batch, see tips.

Ingredients

5 pounds ground beef

2 large onions, finely chopped

2 large green peppers, finely chopped

4 large cloves garlic, minced

1 tablespoon salt

2 teaspoons black pepper

½ teaspoon cayenne pepper

3 tablespoons Worcestershire Sauce

4 tablespoons A-1 Steak Sauce

3 teaspoons oregano

1 small handful fresh parsley, chopped

2 cans (#2½) whole tomatoes, crushed, include juice in sauce

2 large cans tomato puree

2 cups tomato juice

3 cups burgundy wine

Directions

Brown ground beef in cast iron skillet. *(Cook in one-pound batches with portions of the onions, peppers, and garlic in each batch.)*

Place in large, heavy-duty simmering pot.

Add all remaining ingredients to large pot.

Bring to boil - stirring so it doesn't burn.

Reduce heat to simmer - cook for 4 hours, or until cooked down to thick sauce consistency – stir occasionally.

Salt and pepper to taste. *(Be careful not to over-season. you can always add seasoning when you use the sauce.)*

The sauce is perfect for lasagna casserole or spaghetti dinner.

Yield: Sauce for 3 or 4 lasagna casseroles or spaghetti main dish

Recipe Tips

This is enough sauce for 4 or 5 lasagna casseroles or spaghetti dinners. As a rule, I use one batch the day I make the sauce and freeze the rest in air-tight containers for future use.

When ready to reheat - thaw; add a little red wine and season to taste.

Tomato Cream Sauce

Choose your family's favorite type of pasta, cook, and serve. This is quick and easy and the kids will love it!

Ingredients

2 tablespoons olive oil

1 medium onion, finely diced

1 medium to large clove garlic, minced

1 can (28 ounces) diced tomatoes – with juice

1 tablespoon dried basil leaves

1 teaspoon sugar

1 teaspoon dried oregano

1 teaspoon salt

½ teaspoon freshly-ground pepper (adjust to taste)

1 cup heavy cream

1 tablespoon butter (do not use margarine)

Directions

Sauté onion and garlic in olive oil over medium heat - do not burn.

Add all remaining ingredients except cream and butter.

Bring mixture to a boil and cook for 5 minutes or until liquid evaporates.

Remove from heat and stir in heavy cream and butter - mix thoroughly until butter is mostly melted.

Return pan to stove on reduced heat and cook for 5 minutes more.

Serve with pasta of your choice - sprinkle with chopped parsley and parmesan cheese.

Servings: 4

Nancy N Wilson, an Arizona native, has enjoyed tremendous opportunities both personally and professionally. She has lived and worked on both the East Coast and West Coast of the United States; consulted with major corporations in Europe and Japan; and traveled extensively throughout Central and South America.

In 2007, she returned to Arizona to live nearer her two sons and to do what she has always wanted to do – WRITE. Her primary goal was to become a published author. She has now realized that dream and hopes to be writing and publishing for many years to come.

All of the cookbooks in the *Mama's Legacy Series* are listed on the following page, plus her two "how to" cookbooks, *Candy Making Made Easy – Instructions and 17 Starter Recipes* and *Cake Making Made Easy – Instructions and 60 Cakes.* They can be purchased through Amazon.com, The Kindle Store. For easy purchase, simply type each title in the search bar on Amazon.com – or look them all up at once by searching for *Mama's Legacy Series.*

Get your copies today!

Other Books by this Author

Cookbooks

Candy Making Made Easy
Instructions and 17 Starter Recipes

Cake Making Made Easy
Instructions and 60 Cakes

Mama's Legacy Series

Seven Volumes Available
Dinner – 55 Easy Recipes (Volume I)
Breakfast and Brunch – 60 Delicious Recipes (Volume II)
Dessert – 50 Scrumptious Choices (Volume III)
Chicken – 25 Classic Dinners (Volume IV)
Mexican Favorites – 21 Traditional Recipes (Volume V)
Side Dish Recipes (Volume VI)
Sauce Recipes – 50 Tasty Choices (Volume VII)

Health and Fitness
DETOX – The Master Cleanse Diet

Business
Attitude Adjustment

Printed in Great Britain
by Amazon.co.uk, Ltd.,
Marston Gate.